# *Challenging Lifestyle Manual*

Alpha Resources
Alpha North America

Published in North America by Alpha North America, 74 Trinity Place, New York, NY 10006.



ISBN: 1-931808-333

1 2 3 4 5 6 7 8 9 10 Printing/Year 07 06 05 04 03 02

# Contents

# 1

# How to Live under God's Blessing

*Matthew 5:1-6*

## Introduction

The place

The people

The purpose

The passion

Right at the start Jesus teaches us about what matters most in life—not what we have or what we do but who we are

Eight "beautiful attitudes"

The first four are about our relationship with God

## I. "Blessed are the poor in spirit" (v.3)

Dependent on others for support: the opposite of spiritual pride

To recognize how far short we fall of God's standard

To beg for God's mercy, i.e., tax collector (Luke 18:13)

Notes

Notes

## II. "Blessed are those who mourn" (v.4)

It is not wrong to weep and mourn (Ecclesiastes 3:1, 4)

Jesus (John 11) and Paul (Philippians 3:18)

Here the focus is on weeping at our own poverty of spirit

Peter (Matthew 26:75)

## III. "Blessed are the meek" (v.5)

Not weak, spineless, feeble, lifeless or dull, but gentle, considerate and unassuming

Strength under submission to God

Moses (Numbers 12:3, rsv)

## IV. "Blessed are those who hunger and thirst for righteousness" (v.6)

A consuming passion, a grand desire and an overwhelming ambition

A longing to live in a right relationship with God and other people

When we are really desperate God fills and satisfies our desire

## Conclusion

People who follow each of these steps in their relationships with God will live under God's blessing

# 2

# *How to Have an Influence on Society*

*Matthew 5:7-16*

## *Introduction*

Moral vacuum and spiritual hunger in society

Conflict between *"the narrow confines of our own existence"* and *"the broader concerns of humanity"* (Martin Luther King)

Jesus tells a small group of ordinary people that they can have an influence on the entire world

The second four beatitudes concern our relationships with other people

## *I. "Blessed are the merciful" (v.7)*

- ◆To those who are in need: the hungry, sick, outcast, unpopular or lonely
- ◆To those who have wronged us

Those who show mercy will receive mercy

The fact that we forgive is evidence that we have been forgiven

**Notes**

## Notes

by God (Luke 7:47)

A virtuous circle

How much has God forgiven us? (Matthew 18:23-35)

## *II. "BLESSED ARE THE PURE IN HEART" (V.8)*

God looks at the heart, not the outward appearance (1 Samuel 16:7; Mark 7:1-23)

- ◆Being ourselves as God intended, instead of play acting
- ◆Completely sincere

God will reveal himself face to face to the pure

## *III. "BLESSED ARE THE PEACEMAKERS" (V.9)*

- ◆Inner peace
- ◆Peace between people
- ◆Peace with God

## *IV. "BLESSED ARE THOSE WHO ARE PERSECUTED BECAUSE OF RIGHTEOUSNESS" (V.10)*

Jesus never guaranteed popularity

Do not seek persecution, but when it comes regard it as a blessing

Three reasons to *"rejoice and be glad"* (v.12)

◆Because our reward is in heaven (v.12)

◆We identify with Jesus (v.11)

◆Our faith is proved genuine (v.12)

### *V. SUMMARY OF EIGHT STEPS (CHAPTERS 1 AND 2)*

◆Crying out, *"O God, have mercy"*

◆Weeping over our condition

◆Being so broken as to be willing to accept any criticism

◆Being not only desperate about the past, but longing to do something about the future

◆Knowing our own need and being merciful to others

◆Complete openness

◆Blessing others in every possible way

◆Expecting nothing in return, except persecution

Jesus tells this small group of ordinary people that if they live like that they will have an enormous influence on the world around them

**Notes**

Notes

## *Conclusion: Jesus' Application (vv.13-16)*

1) Christians are:

◆*"The salt of the earth"* (v.13)

◆*"The light of the world"* (v.14)

2) Christians must not withdraw from the world into

a Christian sub-culture but get involved in our society

◆At work

◆In our neighborhoods

◆In our leisure activities

◆In politics

◆To fight for justice and freedom

The whole world has massive needs

3) We, as Christians, must remain distinctive from the secular world just as light is different from darkness

Radically different lifestyle:

◆loving God

◆loving our neighbors (see Galatians 5:22-23)

4) Our influence:

Our Christianity

is not only to be expressed in private, (i.e., praying, fasting and giving) but also in public

Jesus proclaimed the gospel, healed the sick, raised the dead, set the captives free and fed the hungry

(see Luke 4:18-21)

> *"Let your light shine before men, that they may see your good deeds and praise your Father in heaven"* (v.16)

## Notes

Notes

# 3
# HOW TO UNDERSTAND THE OLD TESTAMENT
*Matthew 5:17-20*

## INTRODUCTION

Jesus stamped the entire Old Testament with his seal of authority (vv.17, 18)

- ◆(John 10:35) (Matthew 19:4, 5)
- ◆He read it, quoted it, believed it and lived by it

2) Three main ways to look at the Old Testament

- ◆History
- ◆Promise
- ◆Law

## I. JESUS FULFILLS SALVATION HISTORY

1) History is "his story"

a) Matthew begins his gospel, not with the birth of Jesus, but with Jesus' ancestry - the Old Testament story

b) Jesus completes the Old Testament story

(Matthew 1:1-17)

c) Three equal periods between events

◆Fourteen generations from Abraham to David

◆Fourteen generations from David to the Exile

◆Fourteen generations from the Exile to Christ

d) Jesus acquired his identity and mission from the Old Testament story

e) Jesus gave the story significance and authority

2) How then are we to understand the Old Testament?

a) The reality of the Old Testament story is,affirmed

◆A real revelation of God

◆A real relationship between God and his people

b) Jesus sheds light backwards on the story

◆The Old Testament cannot be fully understood without Jesus (John 5:39-40)

◆*"The new is in the old concealed. The old is in the new revealed."* (St. Augustine)

c) Seeing the earlier dealings of God with mankind helps us toward a fuller understanding of Christ

## Notes

Notes

## *II. Jesus fulfills God's promise*

(Matthew 1:18–4:14)

Matthew moves on to Jesus' fulfillment of Old Testament prophecy

The conception, birth and early childhood of Jesus (Matthew 1:22; 2:5, 6, 17, 23; 4:15)

Jesus' birth, life, miracles, betrayal, suffering, death, burial, resurrection, ascension and the outpouring of the Spirit are all predicted in the Old Testament (see Luke 24:27)

The Old Testament is more than a series of predictions: it is a "covenant" (promise) between God and his people

New covenant made in the life, death and resurrection of Jesus

The Old Testament promises are not always fulfilled in the literal form originally given

The fulfillment in terms of what God did in Christ far surpasses the original promise

## *III. Jesus fulfills God's law*

Jesus himself refers to the Old Testament as "the law"

- ◆Jesus reveals the full depth and meaning of the Old Testament law (v.18)

- ◆Jesus fulfilled the Old Testament law in the sense that he lived it out
- ◆Jesus made it possible for us to live a righteous life (Romans 3:21-26; 8:3-4)

## *Conclusion*

Jesus endorsed and fulfilled Old Testament prophecy

> *"The Old Testament tells the story which Jesus completed. It declares the promise which he fulfilled. It provides the pictures and models which shaped his identity. It programs a mission which he accepted and passed on. It teaches the moral orientation to God and the world which he endorsed, sharpened and laid as the foundation for obedient discipleship."*
>
> (Chris Wright: "Knowing Jesus through the Old Testament")

**Notes**

Notes

# 4
# How to Deal With Anger
*Matthew 5:21-26*

## Introduction

What is the extent of the command *"You shall not murder"*? (Exodus 20:13)

Jesus traces "murder" back to the human heart, where the thought processes which lead to the physical act of murder begin

## I. Angry feelings (vv.21, 22)

Old Testament - twenty different words for "wrath" - used 580 times altogether

*"Righteous anger"* is God's personal reaction to sin

- Jesus himself was angry with sin and injustice. (Matthew 21:12, Matthew 23:17, Mark 3:1, 6) But not in selfish reaction to infringement of personal liberty
- When arrested, unfairly tried, tortured and crucified, *"he did not retaliate; when he suffered, he made no threats"* (1 Peter 2:23), rather, *"Father, forgive..."* (Luke 23:34)

Natural feelings can be channelled in a constructive way

Much of our anger is selfish rather than loving anger (Ephesians 4:26)

We do not have any right to feel angry when we are frustrated, disheartened or hurt because we have laid down this right as Jesus did

The "anger that broods, refuses to be pacified and seeks revenge" (translation of Greek) is accountable in heaven (v.22)

Murder begins with angry feelings, then if they are nursed, hatred follows, and if unchecked, the fruit is sometimes actual murder

(See also 1 John 3:15)

Deal with sin at its root

## *II. Angry words (v.22)*

1) Difference between positive outlets for our feelings and unbridled expressions of anger is small

- ◆"Raca": contempt for a person's mind
- ◆"Fool": contempt for heart or character
- ◆These are the lightest terms of abuse, yet they are dangerous
- ◆Angry words pierce the heart

**Notes**

## Notes

2) Loving confrontation and constructive criticism necessary and healthy. Children need discipline

- ◆Truth more important than superficial peace
- ◆Jesus is not suggesting suppression of all feelings and emotions, but shows that reacting *in anger* is dangerous
- ◆God judges the heart

## *III. Dealing with anger*

1) Settle out of church

- ◆Disharmony destroys the church

2) Settle out of court (vv.25, 26)

- ◆"settle matters quickly..." (v. 25)
- ◆Reconciliation: positive steps to restore relationships (vv.23, 24)
- ◆Worship and conduct are inextricably linked

### *Conclusion*

Jesus' standards

Our weaknesses

His mercy and forgiveness

Our determination to deal with anger

His strength for us

# 5

# How to Avoid Sexual Sin

*Matthew 5:27-30*

## *Introduction*

Society's emphasis on sexual fulfillment

Contrary to biblical view of marriage

Family life is the basic structure of society as God intended it to be

God designed sex to cement the relationship of marriage

Brings about a union which is not just physical and biological, but emotional, psychological, spiritual and social

Adultery is sexual intercourse with a person who is not one's spouse

Serious because of the damage it does to all parties involved. Resulting breakdown in family life unravelling fabric of our society

Jesus shows that this sin is not confined to the physical act during an existing marriage: the seventh commandment can also be broken in the heart and mind

**Notes**

Notes

## *I. What is lust? (v.27, 28)*

Jesus intensifies and sharpens the seventh commandment (v.28)

Jesus concerned not only with actions and deeds, but with thoughts and desires

Even if our conduct is outwardly moral and correct we can be guilty of adultery in our thoughts, hearts and imagination

Chain of sin starts in the mind

Nothing wrong with the appreciation of a person's beauty

Nor is Jesus outlawing the natural and normal human desires and attractions which are part of our instinct and nature

Jesus warns that uncontrolled and consuming sexual passion is a road that leads to hell (v.29, 30)

Our thoughts can lead to actions and eventually to a pattern of life which could lead to hell

## *II. How do we avoid lust? (vv.29, 30)*

1) Jesus urges us to take extreme action in order to deal with sin

- ◆Sexual sin is not necessarily the most serious of all sins
- ◆Verses are not about *"literal physical maiming, but ruthless moral self-denial"* (John Stott)

2) Three areas where great self-control may be required

- ◆The eyes (Job 31:1, 7, 9, 11, 12)
- ◆Our hands (v.30)
- ◆Our feet (Matthew 18:8)

## *III. WHAT HAPPENS IF WE FAIL?*

- ◆Repent (Psalm 51)
- ◆Receive forgiveness (2 Samuel 11-12)
- ◆Resist and run (1 Peter 5:8; Genesis 39:1-12)
- ◆Relate
- ◆Recommit to Christ and his service
- ◆Be refilled (Galatians 5:16; Romans 8:13)
- ◆Realize what we are missing

## *CONCLUSION*

When we harbor lust, we limit our own intimacy with God

"The love he offers is so transcendent and possessing that it requires our faculties to be purified and cleansed before we can possibly contain it"

**Notes**

Notes

# 6
# How to Avoid Divorce
## *Matthew 5:31-32; 19:3-11*

### *Introduction*

The issue of divorce and remarriage is complex and controversial, painful and stressful

In rabbinic law, a man had the right to divorce his wife, but the woman had no such right to divorce her husband

Two schools of thought:

- ◆Rabbi Shammai: only divorce for a serious sexual offence
- ◆Rabbi Hillel: *"for any and every reason"*

Pharisees asked Jesus, in effect, whether he agreed with Hillel's view (Matthew 19:3-11)

Four questions arising from teaching of Jesus

### *I. What makes a marriage?*

1) Secular world: marriage is self-chosen, self-created, self-sustained and terminable at will

2) Jesus' view of marriage (Matthew 19:4-6)

- ◆Marriage involves one man and one woman for life
- ◆Leaving parents
- ◆Uniting and a personal commitment
- ◆The *"two will become one flesh"*

*"What God has joined together, let man not separate"*

The fundamental rule is that marriage is permanent and divorce should be ruled out, not because marriage cannot be broken, but because it *ought not to be broken*

## *II. WHAT BREAKS A MARRIAGE?*

Pharisees misquoted

(Deuteronomy 24:1; Matthew 19:7)

Divorce was not a command but a concession

God did not originally intend marriage to end in divorce: *"I hate divorce"* (Malachi 2:16)

The equivalent of adultery (Matthew 19:9; 5:32)

One exception: *"marital unfaithfulness"* (porneia) (Matthew 19:9)

What did he mean by this?

**Notes**

Notes

- ◆A marriage contracted within the prohibited degrees of kinship (Leviticus 18:6-18) would be no marriage at all, and Jesus therefore prohibits
- ◆Fornication before marriage, more commonly taken to include adultery. Old Testament penalty was death (Deuteronomy 22:20-22)

Divorce in recognition that marriage had effectively been terminated

Jesus is affirming the permanence of marriage. Only in the most extreme cases can a marriage be ended

Not to be interpreted with Pharisaic literalism - one act of adultery as biblical grounds for divorce

Jesus' disciples surprised by his strictness (Matthew 19:10)

Tearing apart what God has joined together will inevitably cause damage to at least one of the partners (probably both) and also to the children involved

## *III. Is it ever right for divorced Christians to remarry?*

1) Is a marriage indissoluble until the death of one of the parties?

- ◆Deuteronomy 24:1-4 does

contemplate the possibility of remarriage

- In the society of Jesus' day it was generally assumed that divorced people would remarry (see Matthew 5:32)
- Practically all cultures in the ancient world understood that divorce carried with it the permission to remarry
- Those who take the indissolublists' line end up with an inconsistent position

Even if the partners are free to remarry, in some cases it may not be right to do so

2) Remarriage in church?

Church has a dual role

- Prophetic role to witness to the permanence of marriage
- Pastoral role to witness to the possibility of forgiveness and a new start

## *IV. How are we to respond?*

1) Those already divorced

- Giving and receiving of forgiveness is the key
- Divorce is not an unforgivable sin
- Accept that the marriage is over, but in Christ the guilt can be removed, and that there is now a freedom to start again

**Notes**

## Notes

2) Those who are married

- ◆Do all we can to avoid divorce
- ◆Even if the process of divorce has begun, it is never too late to explore every possibility of reconciliation
- ◆Get help early
- ◆Build strong marriages
- ◆Regular and intimate communication

3) Those who are unmarried

- ◆Singleness is not a curse but a blessing
- ◆An opportunity to accomplish much in life without distractions and the inevitable giving of time and energy to a spouse and family
- ◆Care in the choice of marriage partner

### *Conclusion*

We need to model strong marriages to the world

The most powerful witness to Christ is the different quality of our lives, our relationships and especially our marriages

Draw alongside those facing marriage problems with compassion and understanding, without being judgemental

The heart of the gospel is reconciliation

# 7
# HOW TO LIVE AND ACT WITH INTEGRITY
## *Matthew 5:33-37*

### *INTRODUCTION*

The society into which Jesus was speaking was just as dishonest as ours

The third commandment (Exodus 20:7)

Practical example of how Christians can live righteous lives and be salt and light in society

### *I. INTEGRITY WAS PART OF GOD'S PLAN FOR SOCIETY (V.33)*

1) Summary of extensive Old Testament teaching on the subject of oath taking

- ◆Intended to stop lying and prevent chaos caused when people cannot rely on others' words
- ◆Leviticus 19:11-12;
  Numbers 30:2;
  Exodus 20:7;
  Deuteronomy 23:21-23;
  Numbers 5:19;
  Psalm 50:14;
  Ecclesiates 5:4-5

Notes

Notes

- Integrity involves everything we do and say (vv.34-36)
- Instead of inspiring integrity, oaths became a breeding ground for corruption: people used loopholes to break their commitment without repercussions

2) Jesus confronts the whole system: it is not a question of bringing God in; you cannot keep him out (vv.34-35; Isaiah 66:1; Psalm 48:2)

- (Matthew 23:16-22)
- Whether or not God is named, he is there. He is everywhere
- Life cannot be divided into compartments - those where God is involved and those where he is not
- Our words and our lives should be consistent, wherever we are

## *II. Integrity is a mark of Christian discipleship (v.37)*

1) Jesus goes back to the original purpose behind the law

- Prohibition given since the whole system of oath-taking had become corrupt and was being used to avoid telling the truth (the result of sinful human nature and wickedness in the world) (see James 5:12)

2) Honest people do not need to use oaths: our yes must be yes and our no must be no

- ◆Speak the truth on all occasions

3) Are all oaths and vows prohibited to Christians?

- ◆Oath in a court of law not excluded (see Matthew 26:63, 64)
- ◆Oaths in themselves are not sinful (Hebrews 6:16, 17)
- ◆Jesus is not outlawing, for example, the marriage vows

## *Conclusion*

Christians should be known for their truthfulness, reliability and trustworthiness in their homes, personal relationships and work

We are called to have a righteousness that *"surpasses that of the Pharisees and the teachers of the law"* (Matthew 5:20)

## Notes

Notes

# 8
# How to Respond to Evil People

*Matthew 5:38-42*

## Introduction

Jesus made the most extraordinary demand of his disciples: *"Do not resist an evil person"* (v.39)

How should we respond when we are wronged?

## I. What did the Old Testament teach? (v.38)

Jesus is attacking scribal misinterpretation and wrong application of the law

Lex Talionis: the law of "tit for tat"

- ◆Part of the code of Hammurabi, who reigned in Babylon 2288 - 2242 BC
- ◆Part of the civil law of Israel (Exodus 21:23-25; Leviticus 24:19, 20; Deuteronomy 19:21)

## *II. How should the Old Testament have been interpreted and applied?*

Four qualifications in relation to the Old Testament law:

1) Law of mercy

Designed to rule out escalating revenge

2) Designed for judges not private individuals

(Deuteronomy 19:18-21)

3) Never literal except in the case of capital offenses

Penalties were generally replaced by financial fines

4) Not the whole picture

Individuals were taught not to seek revenge or to bear grudges

(Leviticus 19:18; Proverbs 24:29)

## *III. What did Jesus teach? (vv.39-42)*

Interpreters had turned a restraining injunction into a retributive one

Jesus is not repealing the law but fulfilling it (Matthew 5:17-20)

Unforgiving and vengeful attitude forbidden

Four examples of non-retaliation to loss:

**Notes**

## Notes

1) Loss of pride (v.39)

- ◆Jewish rabbinic law - a back-handed slap (on the right cheek) was twice as insulting as one with the flat of the hand (on the left)
- ◆Jesus himself endured such assaults on more than one occasion (Mark 14:65; John 18:22; 19:3)

2) Loss of possessions (v.40)

- ◆A cloak was valuable and essential. It was a man's inalienable possession (Exodus 22:26; Deuteronomy 24:13)
- ◆Jesus encourages us not only to give up inessentials without opposition but to add even that which we consider essential

3) Loss of time (v.41)

- ◆Romans used to compel citizens to supply food or carry baggage for them (see Matthew 27:32)
- ◆We are not to respond to evil with a vengeful attitude, but to offer to do even more

4) Loss of money (v.42)

- ◆Old Testament taught generosity to the poor (Deuteronomy 15:7, 8, 10, 11)
- ◆Jesus teaches us to put the needs of others before our own. To give to those who will never pay us back

## *IV. How should the teaching of Jesus be interpreted and applied?*

1) Pharisees interpreted the teaching in this area in a very literal way: became legalistic

- ◆Failed to look at the spirit behind the law

2) Jesus is not teaching a new set of literal rules, but a new attitude

- ◆We too must not exalt the letter at the expense of principle
- ◆It is possible to turn the other cheek in a provocative manner

3) To interpret it absolutely literally would be contrary to common sense

The Christian is not *"a doormat...rather the strong man whose control of himself and love for others are so powerful that he rejects absolutely every conceivable form of retaliation"* (John Stott)

4) To interpret it literally would be contrary to the life and teaching of Jesus and the rest of the New Testament

- ◆Jesus' life: John 2:13-16; Matthew 23; John 18:23
- ◆Paul's life: Acts 16:37; Acts 22:25; Acts 25:8-12

**Notes**

## Notes

◆Paul's teaching: (Romans 13:4; Romans 12:17-19)

◆Principle of love lies behind both

5) Criminal wrongs

◆To stand by and allow murder and violence would be unloving and unChristian

◆Our duty as citizens may involve us in the use of force to restrain evil people, i.e., soldier, police officer, judge, anybody

◆We are all private individuals with a command from Jesus not to retaliate or take revenge

◆We are also all citizens of the state with a duty to prevent crime and bring wrongdoers to justice

◆Inevitable tension

6) Civil wrongs

◆Not wrong to go to court, provided our motive is love and justice rather than retaliation and revenge

◆An evil and oppressive employer may need stopping in his tracks. Similarly, it might not be loving to give money to those who we know will use it to abuse their own bodies with alcohol or drugs

◆Check motives

## *Conclusion*

- ◆We must feel the challenge of the words of Jesus and not allow his words to die the death of a thousand qualifications
- ◆We must never allow ourselves to be motivated by revenge or malice
- ◆We are to be generous with our time, money and resources
- ◆We must disregard totally our own rights and combine this with a passionate concern for the rights of others
- ◆We must follow Jesus' example on the cross. He showed how only such an attitude can ultimately triumph over evil

**Notes**

## Notes

# 9
# How to Love Your Enemies
*Matthew 5:43-48*

### Introduction

First time that the word *"love"* has been mentioned

The command, *"Love your neighbor"* (Leviticus 19:18), was wrongly interpreted as being limited to other Jews

No Old Testament warrant for such an attitude

(Exodus 23:4, 5; Deuteronomy 22:1-4; Proverbs 25:21)

We are to love our enemies, regardless of race, color, creed or background and regardless of what harm they have done us

### I. What does it mean to love our enemies? (v.44b)

Some late manuscripts *"love your enemies, bless those who curse you, do good to those who hate you"*

- ◆By our words

  Reply to insults with compliments (Proverbs 15:1)

- ◆By our deeds

*"Do good to those who hate you"*
(Luke 6:27; Proverbs 25:21)

◆By our prayers

Reveals the true feelings in the depth of our hearts which words can sometimes cover over

## *II. WHY SHOULD WE LOVE OUR ENEMIES LIKE THIS?*

1) Common sense suggests:

◆hate multiplies hate

Only love breaks the vicious circle of quarelling, unkindness and misery

◆hate is self-destructive

Hate scars the soul, distorts the personality and wastes our time

◆love is the way to transform an enemy into a friend

2) Yet Jesus gives two quite different reasons:

◆to love our enemies is to imitate our Father in heaven (v.45)

God's love extends even to those who are hostile toward him

◆it is love like this that marks us out from the world (vv.46, 47)

Even unbelievers aren't *"friendly to friends"* (Living Bible)

**Notes**

## Notes

Do the *"extraordinary... the hallmark of the Christian"* (Dietrich Bonhoeffer)

## *Conclusion*

Jesus' own example: enormous strength and courage in the face of appalling cruelty and unjust suffering (Luke 23:34)

Jesus concludes this section of the Sermon with an all-embracing demand:

*"Be perfect, therefore, as your heavenly Father is perfect"* (v.48)

Six examples have been given:

- ◆anger
- ◆lust
- ◆marriage
- ◆integrity
- ◆what to do when wronged
- ◆loving our enemies

An impossible ideal?

Greek: "having attained the intended purpose, complete, full-grown, mature, fully-developed"

Whole-hearted devotion to:

- ◆imitating our Father in heaven
- ◆being different from the world around us
- ◆following the example of Jesus

# 10
# How to Give
## *Matthew 6:1-4*

### *Introduction*

It is the strength of our unseen relationship with God that will decide whether or not we have strong, healthy Christian lives

Emphasis shifts from love for neighbor to love for God (Matthew 22:37-39)

Three pillars of contemporary Jewish piety were:

- ◆giving
- ◆praying
- ◆fasting

Jesus teaches how and why his followers should act in contrast with:

- ◆the Pharisees (hypocrites) (vv.2, 5, 16) They liked everyone to see how religious they were
- ◆the irreligious (pagans) (v.7). Had no real relationship with God: *"mechanical formalism"* (John Stott)

Followers of Jesus are to be unlike both of these, who *"have received their reward in full"* (v.3)

This section (dealing with giving, prayer and fasting) is introduced by a general command

**Notes**

## Notes

*"Be careful not to do your 'acts of righteousness' before men, to be seen by them. If you do, you will have no reward from your Father in heaven."* (v.1)

The rest of the section is a commentary on this verse

Our motive for living out the Christian life should be the glory of God

Christian activity might be seen, but it must never be done for the sake of being seen

### I. How not to give (v.2)

1) A devout Jew would give in two ways:

- ◆by tithe, one tenth of his income (compulsory)
- ◆by giving alms (voluntary)

2) In total a devout Jew would give at least one sixth of his income (the most sacred of all religious duties)

3) If we give in order to get *"honor from men"* we will receive no more honor than that (v.2)

### II. How to give (vv.3-4)

Figurative language expresses the need for secrecy (v.3)

The result of an overflowing love and kindness of heart, a joy and delight (2 Corinthians 9:7)

Reward from God (v.4)

## *Conclusion*

Issue of rewards: proper rewards are *"the activity itself in consummation."* (C.S.Lewis)

What are the rewards of giving?

(2 Corinthians 9:6-15)

- ◆Giving is the best investment we can make (v.6)
- ◆We will know God's love (v.7)

  No rules about how much we should give, only that it should be a generous proportion of what we have
- ◆Giving frees us from financial worry (v.8)

  Handing over the burden and the worry, not the responsibility itself
- ◆Giving transforms our whole character (v.10)

  Frees us from materialism
- ◆We have the joy of seeing others giving thanks and praise to God as a result (v.11)
- ◆We have the joy and satisfaction of *"supplying the needs of God's people"* (2 Corinthians 9:12)
- ◆We are doing what Jesus did (2 Corinthians 9:15)

  He was rich, yet became poor so that we might become rich

**Notes**

## Notes

# 11
# HOW TO PRAY
### *Matthew 6:5-14*

### *INTRODUCTION*

Jewish people prayed regularly

- ◆Twice a day the "Shema"
- ◆Three times a day the "Tephillah"

Jesus gives four guidelines:

### *I. SINCERITY (V.5)*

Not criticizing public worship or corporate prayer: but the motive is important

Right motive for prayer: to encounter our Father in heaven

### *II. SECRECY (V.6)*

No distractions

If we seek the reward or the admiration of others, that is all we will get

If we seek to encounter God, our reward will be great, and include:

- ◆knowing God's love
- ◆joy (Psalm 16:11)
- ◆peace: guilt, burdens, problems unloaded
- ◆new perspective on life

◆guidance: hear his voice

◆see our prayers answered

◆power for living

## *III. SIMPLICITY (VV.7, 8)*

Hypocrites pray from a wrong motive

Pagans pray in a wrong manner. They believed that the longer they prayed the more likely they were to be heard

Quality rather than quantity counts with God

Difference between persistence and mindless repetition: (Luke 11:5-8; Luke 18:1-8)

We do not pray to inform God of something he does not know about (v.8). Rather, God gives us the privilege of being involved in his plans

## *IV. STRUCTURED (VV.9-15)*

The most simple and yet refined model for prayer

It covers in principle everything we could ask of God

We are not to look down on asking as the lowest form of prayer

Supplication is at the very heart of the prayer which Jesus taught his disciples:

◆*"Our Father in heaven"*

The word Jesus used for

**Notes**

## Notes

*"Father"* was *"Abba"*, a word which conveys intimacy

A privilege now opened to us (John 1:12; Galatians 4: 4-6)

Part of God's family, praying with many others

Praise, adoration and thanksgiving as we begin to pray

◆ *"Hallowed be your name"*

The name of God signifies the revelation of who he is

Our first concern should be for God's name to be honored in our country, in our institutions and in our own lives

◆ *"Your kingdom come"*

God's rule and reign to transform every area of society

In addition it is a prayer for his return

◆ *"Your will be done"*

Desire to know God's will and to see God's will done in our lives

◆ *"Give us today our daily bread"*

Basic material needs should be included in our prayers. Nothing is too small to pray about

- *"Forgive us our debts as we also have forgiven our debtors"*

  Jesus enlarges on this (vv.14, 15)

  We do not earn forgiveness by forgiving others, but it is evidence that we have received forgiveness (see Matthew 18:23-35)

- *"And lead us not into temptation, but deliver us from the evil one"*

  God does not tempt us (James 1:13) but allows us to be exposed to the temptations of the devil

  *"Grant that we will not fail the test"*

  We are all tempted and we need God's protection and his power

## Conclusion

When we pray, God always rewards us

## Notes

Notes

# 12
# How to Fast
## *Matthew 6:16-18*

### *Introduction*

1) Third of the secret disciplines

Distinguish:

- ◆hunger-strike: political motivation
- ◆dieting: physical motivation

2) Jesus fasted (Matthew 4:2) and assumed that his disciples would fast

- ◆Not *"you must fast"* (legalistic) or *"if you fast..."* (optional). Rather, *"when you fast..."* (v.16)
- ◆But inappropriate for his disciples as long as he was with them (Matthew 9:14, 15; Mark 2:18-20, Luke 5:33, 34)
- ◆Later, when he was no longer with them, it would be right and proper for them to fast (i.e., Acts 13: 2, 3, 14:23; 2 Corinthians 11:27; 6:5; 1 Corinthians 9:27)

### *I. Why should we fast?*

1) As with giving and praying, Jesus promises that those who fast in the right way will receive

reward from God (v.18)

a) To reinforce prayer

◆(Ezra 8:21, 23; Judges 20)

◆People who pray with fasting are giving notice that they are really in earnest

◆(Jonah 3:5, 10; Mark 9:29)

b) Sign of repentance and humility before God

◆(Psalm 35:13; Joel 2:12)

◆Personal sin (2 Samuel 12:16-23)

◆National sin (Daniel 9:3)

◆(1 Samuel 7:6; Nehemiah 9:1, 2)

c) Guidance

◆(Exodus 34:28; Deuteronomy 9:9; Jehoshaphat - 2 Chronicles 20: 3, 4)

◆New Testament church (Acts 13, 14:23)

d) Self-discipline (1 Corinthians 9:24-27)

◆Fasting helps to lessen the hold of material things upon us

e) Share with hungry (Isaiah 58:6, 7, 10)

## *II. Why not?*

Modern objections to fasting - three main objections:

a) Theological (Matthew 9:14, 15; Acts 13:2, 3;

**Notes**

Notes

Matthew 25:6)

b) Historical

◆Reaction to asceticism of the Middle Ages

◆Opposite of abuse is not disuse but right use

c) Practical

◆Some argue that fasting is unhealthy

◆Not sensible for:

- Those who are pregnant or breast-feeding
- For a diabetic or someone who has a member of the family who is diabetic
- Those who are convalescing from surgery or illness or taking medication
- Those who are stressed, depressed or suffering from bereavement
- Those liable to eating disorders

For most people it is a benefit to our health: detoxifies the system, cleansing and resting vital organs such as the kidneys and the liver

## *III. How should we fast?*

The blessings of fasting are not automatic

(Isaiah 58:2-12; Jeremiah 14: 11, 12; Zechariah 7)

1) Not ostentatious like *"the hypocrites"*

- ◆Not gloomy-faced

2) Be sensible

- ◆Start on short fast
- ◆Prepare beforehand
- ◆Drink a lot of water
- ◆Get rest
- ◆Don't eat too much afterward

3) Avoid legalism

## Conclusion

We should fast out of love for God

Part of our relationship with God to fast when we sense his Spirit asking us to do so

Our fasting should always center on God (Zechariah 7:5)

## Notes

Notes

# 13
# How to Handle Money
## *Matthew 6:19-24*

### Introduction

We prefer not to talk about money in church but Jesus talked about it a great deal

We have a choice to make: Jesus puts it in three different ways

### I. Where is our security? (vv.19-21)

*"Treasure"* can be stored on earth or in heaven

Our hearts will follow our treasure

Treasure is not only money, but anything we hold dear. Earthly treasure will not last (v.20)

1) Often misunderstood and misinterpreted

- a) All Christians are not required to give away all they have
  - Only one recorded case (Mark 10:21)
  - It seems that Nicodemus and Joseph of Arimathea continued

to be wealthy after becoming disciples of Jesus

- During his ministry, Jesus was supported by wealthy women (Luke 8:1-3)

b) It is not wrong to make money

Parable of the talents

Some are called to make money for the glory of God and for use in his kingdom

Some may be called to positions of power, wealth and influence

c) It is not wrong to save

Provide for our relatives (1 Timothy 5:8; Mark 7:9-12)

Enables us to provide for the needs of others

d) It is not wrong to enjoy the good things of life (1 Timothy 6:17)

Jesus was neither an ascetic nor indulgent, but his attitude was balanced (Luke 11:37; John 2:1-11; Matthew 11:19)

Wealth, at least in the Old Testament, was often seen as a sign of God's blessing. Under the new covenant, God's blessing is spiritual, but material things can be enjoyed as undeserved gifts from God

## Notes

## Notes

2) Jesus is concerned not so much with our wealth, but with our hearts and affections

a) The very things that promise security lead to perpetual insecurity (v.19)

b) Materialism leads us away from God (v.21)

*"Tethers our hearts to the earth"* (John Stott)

3) We should store treasure in heaven

Not earning our salvation, but investing in the kingdom of heaven - God's rule and reign on the earth

Investing in his kingdom will primarily mean putting our time, energy and money into things such as preaching the gospel, healing the sick, caring for the weak and lonely, and ministering to the poor

4) Two reasons for this

a) This investment is totally secure and will last forever (v.20)
(1 Peter 1:4; 2 Corinthians 4:18; Romans 8:38, 39)

b) Jesus says that our hearts will follow our treasure (v.21)

Once we invest in the kingdom of God we will become a great deal more interested and committed to it

## *II. What is our ambition in life? (vv.22, 23)*

Analogy of physical eyes

Where are our spiritual sights set - on God or on materialism?

Good eyes are fixed on Jesus (Hebrews 12:2)

Bad eyes are fixed on selfish gain and materialism

We are called to be single-minded, setting our thoughts and our sights on Jesus and his kingdom

## *III. Whom do we serve? (v.24)*

1) Money has all the characteristics of a pagan god. It seems to offer security, freedom, power, influence, status and prestige

- It demands sacrifice and, ultimately, human sacrifice
- *"Our hearts have room only for one all-embracing devotion, and we can only cleave to one Lord"* (Dietrich Bonhoeffer)

2) Money is a good servant, but a bad master

- If we serve it we will become a slave to it
- We think we own it but, if we are not careful, it ends up owning us
- *"If you make money your god it will plague you like the devil"* (Henry Fielding)

**Notes**

## Notes

- If money is our god we will *"despise"* (be indifferent to) the only true god (v.24)

## *Conclusion*

Modern society and the delight in riches (Matthew 13:22)

Materialism is atheism: being without God

If we serve God, we must be unconcerned about money: it all belongs to him and we are mere stewards

Hold on to it loosely

Break power of materialism by generous giving. This is an act of the will: saying "no" to mammon and "yes" to God

Generous giving celebrates *"the fact that Jesus is Lord and Mammon isn't"* (N.T.Wright)

# 14
# How to Stop Worrying and Start Living

*Matthew 6:25-34*

## *Introduction*

The pervasiveness of worry in modern society

Jesus' solution is radical. As always, he glossed over the symptoms but went directly to the root cause

## *I. What does he mean?*

1) He does not mean that we should not think about the future

- ◆The book of Proverbs often makes it clear that planning is vital

2) It is not an excuse for idleness

- ◆Jesus did not mean that we need not bother to earn a living
- ◆The *"birds of the air"* work hard, but are free from worry

3) He does not mean that we should not be ambitious

- ◆Ambition is a strong desire to achieve success and con-

**Notes**

Notes

cerns our goals and motivation

4) He is not saying that we should opt out of our responsibilities

◆We need to take responsibility for our own life and for others in society, as one day we will have to give an account for it (2 Corinthians 11:27, 28)

5) He is not saying that we won't have anything to worry about

◆If anyone had cause for worry Jesus did:

- day to day living without a regular source of income
- knew what it was for close friend to die
- misunderstood, threatened with death and unfairly tried
- powerful temptations
- suffering and living his life under the shadow of the cross
- responsibility

## *II. Why are we not to worry?*

1) Jesus' reasons

◆To worry is to miss the point of life (v.25)

◆Worry is illogical (v.26)

- ◆Worry is a waste of time (v.27)
- ◆Worry is incompatible with faith (vv.28-30)
- ◆Worry is not Christian (v.32)
- ◆Worry is unnecessary (v.33)
- ◆Worry is incompatible with common sense (v.34)

## *III. How do we stop worrying?*

1) Get our ambitions, priorities and responsibilities right

2) Seek God's rule and reign:

- ◆in our own lives (marriage, home, family, lifestyle)
- ◆in the lives of others (friends, relations, neighbors, colleagues, community)
- ◆in society (wider needs)

3) Proper investment of:

- ◆time
- ◆money
- ◆energy

## Notes

### *Conclusion*

*"Seek first his kingdom and his righteousness, and all these things will be given to you as well"* (v.33)

This is how to stop worrying and start living

Notes

# 15
# *How to Handle Criticism*
*Matthew 7:1-6*

## *Introduction*

Relationships: how we respond to other people

Not Christians on our own - we belong to a community

Jesus shows how and when to give and receive criticism, how and when to confront others and to discriminate without judging

## *I. The Command: What are we not to do? (v.1)*

1) *"Do not judge"* (v.1)

Jesus' words must be looked at in context

- ◆The immediate setting of the Sermon on the Mount (see v.6 and vv.15-20)
- ◆Jesus' teaching as a whole (see Matthew 10:14-15; 18:15-17)
- ◆The rest of the Bible

2) What does Jesus not mean?

- ◆Not the authority of the state

Pilate had a God-given right to judge (John 19:11)

We need judges (Romans 13:4)

◆Not authority in the home

The book of Proverbs is full of exhortations to parents to exercise authority

◆Not authority in the church

(2 Timothy 4:2;
Galatians 1:8-9; 2:11; 5:12;
1 Corinthians 5;
1 Corinthians 6:1-6)

◆Not the suspension of our critical faculties: we often need to discern

We need to distinguish false from true

We need to make value judgements
(John 7:24; 1 John 4:1;
1 Thessalonians 5:21)

3) What does he mean?

◆Judgemental attitude toward other people

Playing God

Fault finding

Self-righteous attitude (Luke 18:9)

We have Christ's righteousness, not our own, and have no cause for pride (Ephesians 2:8)

We should not patronize non-Christians or, worse still, judge and condemn them

## Notes

Notes

If this applies to those who are not Christians, how much more should it apply to our *"brother"*

## *II. The reason: why are we not to judge? (vv.1, 2)*

1) As we judge, we are judged

So often, as we judge we reveal our own weaknesses

2) We will bring the judgement of others on our own heads

Those who judge must expect similar treatment, leading to environment of judgementalism. Tragedy when this occurs in the church

3) The judgement of God

- ◆No human being is qualified to sit in judgement on another (Romans 2:1-3)
- ◆We are all full of prejudice
- ◆We never know all the facts: God does (1 Corinthians 4:5)
- ◆In due time the Lord will judge (1 Corinthians 4:4, 5)

a) Some rabbis used to teach that God had two measures: a measure of justice and a measure of mercy

b) The measure you give will be the measure you get

c) We are called to love as he loves us. He does not treat us as our sins deserve

d) We should give others the benefit of the doubt and be

forgiving, understanding and loving

## *III. The illustration: what does it mean in practice? (vv.3-5)*

Jesus often referred to the Pharisees as *"blind guides"*

Not ruling out constructive comment, but unkind and hypocritical criticism, even if it takes the form of a kindly act

Hypocrisy is the gap between what we show on the outside and what we know is true on the inside

Speaking ill of others can be a way of dishonestly speaking well of ourselves: morally and doctrinally

We need to start with self-criticism

*"We need to be as critical of ourselves as we often are of others, and as generous to others as we always are to ourselves"* (John Stott)

No accident that Jesus uses the analogy of an eye - no organ more sensitive. Criticism of others is a delicate operation

(2 Timothy 4:2; Matthew 18: 15-17)

## *IV. Qualification: are there any limits? (v.6)*

1) The danger of being indiscriminate

**Notes**

Notes

- ◆We have been entrusted with something sacred
- ◆"Pearls" are the truth and good news of the gospel
  - Dogs: wild hounds
  - Pigs: unclean animals
- ◆Do not feed swine with precious pearls

2) We should not avoid preaching the gospel to unbelievers (that is exactly what he commissioned his followers to do) but beware of those who show *"hardened contempt for God"* (Calvin)

- ◆(Matthew 10:14; Luke 10:10, 11)
- ◆Paul followed this policy (Acts 13:46, Acts 18:6)
- ◆We must learn to accept constructive criticism and advice (Proverbs 25:12)

## *CONCLUSION*

Jesus is urging us to act with love and charity, cutting out petty squabbles and judgementalism:

- ◆toward our fellow human beings
- ◆in our churches
- ◆in the church as a whole

Unity in and around Jesus Christ. God will judge and his judgement will be perfect

# 16
# How to Get our Relationships Right

*Matthew 7:7-12*

## Introduction

Relationships are the most important aspects of our lives

As Jesus reaches the end of the ethical teaching, before the call to commitment, he summarizes all that he has been saying: *"for this sums up the Law and the Prophets"* (v.12) (see Matthew 22:36-40)

## I. How to get our relationship with God right (vv.7-11)

1) The first and greatest commandment is to love God

- Jesus says *"ask...seek...knock"*
- "Present imperative" literally means "to keep on asking, to keep on seeking and to keep on knocking"
- Jeremiah 29:13, 14

2) Three reasons for confidence

## Notes

**Notes**

in our relationship with God

a) God is our *"Father in heaven"* (v.11)

We can use the same language as Jesus when addressing him (*"Abba"* Matthew 6:9)

b) We will not miss out but receive *"good gifts"* (v.11)

c) God will *only* give us good things

God will never give us anything harmful (2 Peter 1:3)

3) Our primary aim in life: to develop a relationship with our loving heavenly Father; to love him; to seek and to receive good gifts from his fatherly hand; to love him with all our heart, mind, soul and strength

## *II. How to get our relationships with other people right (v.12)*

"The golden rule". Many people have taught the 'negative' version of this rule, but Jesus was the first to formulate this rule "positively"

- "Negative" says: *"I won't do anyone any harm"* - allows us to be inactive
- "Positive": not only, *"I won't do anyone any harm"*, but

also, *"I will go out of my way to help them"*

*"For this sums up the Law and the Prophets"* (v.12), not replaces or abolishes them

Details keep us from sentimentalism: general principles keep us from legalism

## *Conclusion*

Such love is only possible as God pours his love on us (1 John 4:19)

If the church lived like this, the world would believe

## Notes

Notes

# 17
# How to Find Life
## *Matthew 7:13-14*

### *Introduction*

Jesus changes from teaching to challenge

Two alternatives - far reaching consequences

### *I. What is the difference?*

1) Two lifestyles (roads):

one "broad"(v.13), the other "narrow" (v.14)

a) The broad road

- ◆No boundaries: you can do what you like
- ◆A life of ease, without having to keep to Jesus' standards
- ◆An easy road, but where there are no boundaries people get hurt

b) The narrow road (v.14)

- ◆Tight boundaries
- ◆Many things are not permitted: many extra things are required (Matthew 7:12)

◆Impossible to keep Jesus' standards without his help, all the way, all the time

## *II. Where do they lead?*

Two destinations: "destruction" (v.13) and "life" (v.14)

Not a threat but a warning given out of love

*"The supernatural life belonging to God and Christ, which the believers will receive in the future, but which they also enjoy here and now"*

(Walter Bauer)

Jesus defines eternal life (John 17:3)

Need for care if comparing the two roads (Psalm 73:13, 17)

## *III. Who is on the roads?*

Two groups of people: "many" (v.13) and a "few" (v.14)

Large crowds can give a false sense of security

The few are not as few as all that (Revelation 7:9)

1900 million Christians in the world today

Only a minority of the world's total population: thus we can often feel alone

**Notes**

Notes

## *IV. How do I get in?*

Two entrances: *"wide"* (v.13) and *"small"* (v.14)

There are many ways in which one could enter through the wide gate

There is only one way through the narrow gate: repentance and faith in Jesus Christ

You cannot take sin in with you

The longer one has been on the wrong road, the harder it is to admit, and to change, although it is never too late to do so

## *Conclusion*

Everyone is on one of the two roads

There is no middle road, no third gate, no neutral group

If we are on the broad road we do not need to do anything in order to stay on it. But if we want to get off it we need to enter the narrow gate through repentance and faith in Jesus Christ

As we enter through the narrow gate, we find that although there may not be huge numbers on the road, we are not alone. Jesus Christ himself goes with us

# 18
# How to Discern False Prophets
*Matthew 7:15-23*

Notes

## Introduction

1) Some attacks on the church are from the outside: persecution

2) Some attacks are from within the church itself: *"false prophets"* (v.15)

- ◆Some might be from a community outside the orthodox body of Christian belief, but who claim to be the true (and only) people of God
- ◆Some might speak from within the mainstream church

Prophet: anyone who speaks "in the name of the Lord"

Enemies of God's people throughout the Bible
Ezekiel 22:27; Zephaniah 3:3; Matthew 10:16; John 10:12; Acts 20:29

3) How are we to spot these false teachers?

## Notes

## *I. The wrong test: looking on the outside*

The wrong test is a superficial one: looking at the outward clothing

Does not work because *"ferocious wolves"* can appear *"in sheep's clothing"* (v.15)

"Sheep's clothing" could include:

- ◆outward profession of faith (v.21)

  Not sufficient to know Christian jargon or recite creeds

- ◆supernatural activity (v.22-23)

  Jesus is not speaking against the activities themselves: He clearly expected that his disciples would *"prophesy"*, *"drive out demons"* and *"perform miracles"*

## *II. The right test: looking on the inside*

*"By their fruit you will recognize them"* (vv.16, 20)

1) Fruit is visible and relatively easy to test (vv.16-19)

- ◆Not roots: they are underground
- ◆A diseased tree cannot produce good fruit
- ◆A tree that is in good condition will produce good fruit

- ◆We should be wise and discerning, but need not worry, since false prophets will reveal themselves

2) The fruit will have at least six features:

a) The fruit of character: who they are

- ◆(Galatians 5:22, 23; Matthew 5:1-16)
- ◆Christian leaders should display these fruits (although no one is perfect)

b) The type of conduct: what they do

- ◆"The will of my Father" (v.21)
- ◆Our creed determines our conduct

c) The content of their teaching: what they say

- ◆(Matthew 12:33-37; Deuteronomy 13:1-3)
- ◆We can test a prophet by his teaching - whether he leads people to God or away from him
- ◆Check against the Bible (Acts 17:11)

d) The style of their relationships: how they love

- ◆(John 15:10-12)
- ◆Set alongside his admonition in the previous section: (Matthew 7:1) be aware of judging and condemning other Christians

## Notes

## Notes

e) The result of their influence: the effect they have

- Is their congregation united in love, full of joy, living in peace, patient, full of kindness to others, doing good, and showing themselves to be faithful, gentle and self-controlled?
- The test of preaching is the effect it has on people
- Not a single member but the congregation as a whole (Luke 6:40)

f) The depth of their relationship with Jesus: who they are in private

- (John 15:1-17)
- "Apart from me you can do nothing" (John 15:5)
- Hence, Jesus will say to the false prophet: *"I never knew you"* (v.23)
- One of the Old Testament tests of a true prophet (Jeremiah 23:18)

## *Conclusion*

The true prophet knows Jesus Christ, listens to him and speaks his word

God has given us his word and his Spirit to enable us to test whether a prophet is genuinely from him

# 19
# How to Build a Secure Future
## *Matthew 7:24-29*

### *Introduction*

The last three sections of the Sermon on the Mount are all about decisions

Finally, Jesus requires us to decide the basis for our lives: rock or sand

Again, only two alternatives. In current climate of pluralism and permissiveness we would like to think that there are many different ways to build our lives

In the previous section he contrasted "doing" and "saying"; in this one he contrasts "doing" and "hearing"

Two men, two houses, two foundations, two results and two responses to Jesus

### *I. Superficial similarities*

1) Both men built a house (vv.24, 26)

Intending long-lasting significance

**Notes**

Notes

2) Bad weather attacked both houses (vv.25, 27)

All face pressures and troubles in this world

The image of *"rain... torrents...winds"* is used elsewhere to refer to God's judgement (Ezekiel 13:11)

3) Both men had the opportunity to respond (vv.24, 26)

- ◆Many people today hear the words of Jesus: at school, at churches or meetings or from an evangelist like Billy Graham
- ◆Hearing is not enough

## *II. Underlying differences*

- Wisdom
- Foundations
- Results

Paul did not avoid life's problems but took the long view (see 2 Corinthians 11:23-28; 4:17-18)

The wise man has much to look forward to: (Revelation 21:1; 21:3; 1 Corinthians 15; 1 Corinthians 2:9)

This life: Ephesians 1:13-14

## *III. The key difference*

Putting Jesus' words into practice (v.24)

1) What Jesus does not mean

We do not earn our way into the kingdom of God by good works

(Matthew 5:3)

Rest of New Testament

We are not sinless (Romans 3:23; 1 John 1:8)

2) What Jesus does mean

Listening alone is not enough: hearing must lead to action

(Romans 2:13; James 1:22-25; 2:14-20; 1 John 1:6; 2:4)

Our theology must affect our lives

Four areas:

- ◆repentance
- ◆faith in Jesus
- ◆our need of the power of the Holy Spirit (Luke 11:13)
- ◆live it out

## *Conclusion*

Those who heard Jesus were *"amazed"* (v.28)

Not second-hand: he was *"not like their teachers of the law"* (v.29)

He did not teach by authority, but taught as one who had authority (v.29)

The Sermon on the Mount is not simply "good moral teaching"

Jesus presents us with a radical, life-transforming challenge - indeed, the ultimate challenge

## Notes

# Notes